THE KIDS' LIBRARY OF MARTIAL ARTS™

KARATE

Pamela Randall

The Rosen Publishing Group's
PowerKids Press™
New York

Published in 1999 by The Rosen Publishing Group, Inc.
29 East 21st Street, New York, NY 10010

First Edition

Book Design: Danielle Primiceri

Photo Illustrations by Seth Dinnerman

Randall, Pamela.
    Karate / by Pamela Randall.
        p. cm. — (The kids' library of martial arts)
    Includes index.
    Summary: Introduces the history, basic moves, and terminology of this martial art.
    ISBN 0-8239-5236-3
    1. Karate—Juvenile literature. [1. Karate.] I. Title. II. Series: Randall, Pamela. The kids' library of martial arts.
    GV1114.3.R362   1998
    796.815'3—dc21   97-49273
                                                                CIP
                                                                AC

Manufactured in the United States of America

Contents

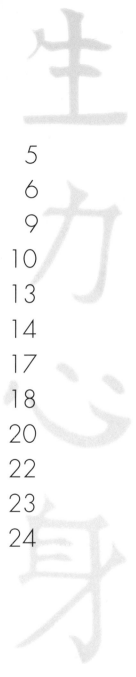

Welcome to the Dojo

Doug and Lisa are new students at the **dojo** (DOH-joh). A dojo is a school where people study **martial arts** (MAR-shul ARTS). Like the other boys and girls in their class, Lisa and Doug hope to learn karate. Lisa wants to study karate so she'll feel more **confident** (KON-fih-dent) around the bigger kids at school. Doug is taking karate because he enjoys all kinds of sports. Grown-ups study karate for many of the same reasons that kids do. But they aren't usually in the same classes as kids.

◄ *It is important to stretch before practicing karate. Being well-stretched makes it easier to do karate moves.*

A Little Bit of History

Karate comes from the Japanese island of **Okinawa** (oh-kih-NAH-wah). It is located almost halfway between China and the main islands of Japan. People going to China or Japan often stopped in Okinawa. This made it a place where traders, soldiers, and local people traded goods as well as ideas about hand-to-hand fighting. In the 1700s, several styles of martial arts were created there. Together, they were known as *Okinawa-te*, or Okinawan hand. In the 1900s, a man named Funakoshi Gichin brought the styles of *Okinawa-te* together and called them karate.

The island of Okinawa is part of a group of islands called the Okinawa Islands. ▶

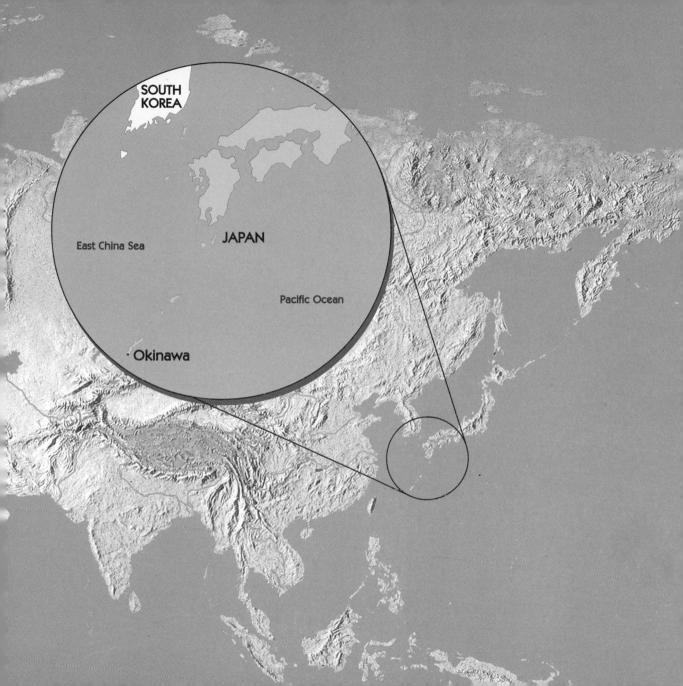

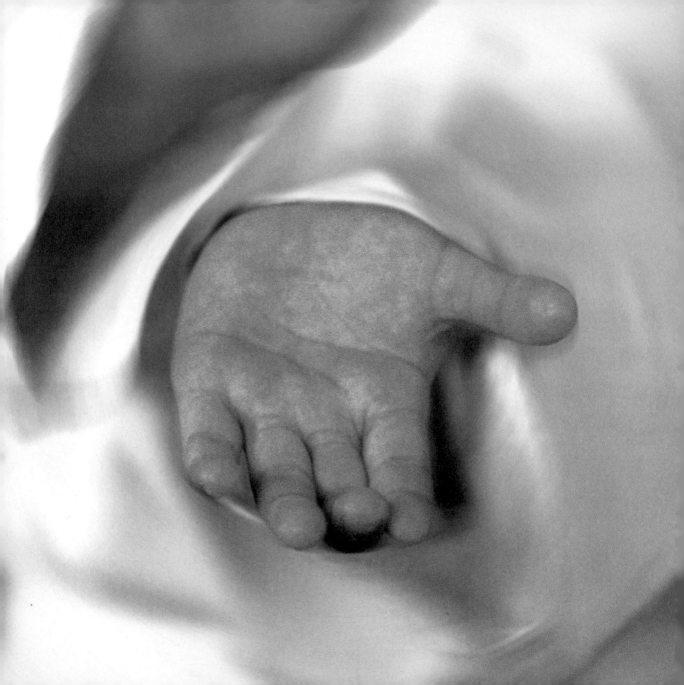

An Empty Hand

Karate is great for **self-defense** (SELF-dih-FENS). Many people also enjoy it as a sport, just as they enjoy football or wrestling. But karate is about a lot more than fighting.

Students of karate are called *karateka* (kuh-rah-TAY-kah). *Karateka* are expected to learn how to stay calm inside and to think clearly. They are also taught to understand themselves well and pay close attention to their **relationships** (rih-LAY-shun-ships) with other people. This helps students apply the beliefs of karate to all parts of their lives.

◀ *In karate, an empty hand is the strongest weapon.*

More Than Fighting

There are forms of martial arts, such as kung fu, that use weapons. Karate does not involve the use of weapons. In fact, the word karate comes from the Japanese characters *kara* which means empty and *te* which means hand. All together, then, karate means empty hand, or fighting without weapons. People who study karate learn ways of attacking an **opponent** (uh-POH-nent) and **defending** (dih-FEN-ding) themselves using only their arms and their legs.

Karate students learn that it is important to have a strong body and a strong mind. ▶

From Fighting to Sport

When modern karate got its start, it was used only for fighting. But as time passed, people began looking for a way to enjoy karate as a sport. They started what became known as **karate-do** (kuh-RAH-tay-DOH). The **suffix** (SUH-fiks) *do* means way. *Karate-do* mixed the moves of karate with a belief in **spiritual** (SPEER-ih-choo-ul) improvement.

In *karate-do*, the *karateka* don't follow through with their movements. They stop short of actually touching their opponents, so no one is hurt.

◀ *When students practice karate, they don't hit their opponent. Instead, they stop just short of making contact.*

Do You Speak Karate?

Even though there are hundreds of styles of karate, there are five schools, or **ryus** (REEYOOZ), that are very popular. They are *Shotokan, Wado Ryu, Goju Ryu, Shito Ryu,* and *Kyokushinkai.*

A karate student's uniform is called a **karate gi** (kuh-RAH-tay GEE). The belt is called an **obi** (OH-bee). The colors of a student's belt change as he or she moves higher in rank, or skill level. Belt colors include white, yellow, orange, green, and brown. Black is the highest rank.

Karate students must practice their moves often if they wish to advance to a higher rank. ▶

Stances Are Important

The way students stand is important in karate. The position they stand in is called a **stance** (STANS). Stances make it harder for students to be thrown off balance by an opponent.

One of the most common stances is the back stance. In this stance, one of Lisa's legs is behind the other, and most of her weight is on the back leg. Her two feet form an L-shape. Both knees are slightly bent.

◀ *Practicing the different stances of karate can help keep students from getting knocked down by their opponents.*

Kicks Are Important

Kicking is an important part of karate. One karate kick is called the front thrust kick. To do this move, Doug stands in a right front stance. This is similar to the right back stance, but most of his weight is on his front foot.

Doug lifts his left leg to the height of his right knee. He pulls his body backward, and then thrusts forward. Doug uses his body's motion to push his foot forward toward his target.

The front thrust kick is just one of the many kinds of kicks there are to learn in karate. ▶

A Hammer with No Nail

Another kind of karate move is called a hammer strike. It is a hand motion. Lisa can do it while she is in any karate stance. She pulls her right hand back in front of her chest. Then she strikes outward and up with that hand.

This karate move has the power of a hammer. But there's no nail!

Looking Ahead

Lisa and Doug enjoy what they are learning at karate school. Lisa will feel safer once she learns to defend herself. She probably won't ever have to use karate for self-defense. But just knowing it gives her more self-confidence. Doug has learned a lot from studying karate too. The new skills he's learning, along with **self-discipline** (SELF-DIH-sih-plin), will keep his body strong and fit.

Glossary

confident (KON-fih-dent) Believing in yourself and your abilities.

defending (dih-FEN-ding) Protecting something against an attack.

dojo (DOH-joh) A place where karate is practiced.

karate-do (kuh-RAH-tay-DOH) A form of karate that is more gentle than karate and can be used for sport.

karate gi (kuh-RAH-tay GEE) The uniform worn when doing karate.

karateka (kuh-rah-TAY-kah) Students of karate.

martial art (MAR-shul ART) Any of the arts of self-defense or fighting that is practiced as sport.

obi (OH-bee) A belt worn in karate that shows a student's rank.

Okinawa (oh-kih-NAH-wah) A Japanese island that is also close to China.

opponent (uh-POH-nent) A person who is on the other side in a fight.

relationship (rih-LAY-shun-ship) A connection, usually with friends and family.

ryu (REEYOO) A school or style of karate.

self-defense (SELF-dih-FENS) To protect yourself against an attack.

self-discipline (SELF-DIH-sih-plin) To make yourself do the things you should.

spiritual (SPEER-ih-choo-ul) Having to do with a person's spirit.

stance (STANS) A position you stand in when you fight.

suffix (SUH-fiks) An ending attached to a word that changes its meaning.

Index

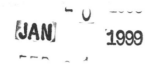